My First Book of Jewish Holidays

Maida Silverman

COLLAGRAPHS BY

Barbara Garrison

Dial Books for Young Readers ☀ New York

The art for this book is a series of collagraphs, a word that comes from "collage" and "graphic." The artist's collagraphs begin with a heavy piece of cardboard. Additional pieces of matboard, paper, fabric, tape, string, etc. are glued onto the cardboard plate; areas of the cardboard may be cut and peeled away. Gesso is painted over the entire area, and Carborundum abrasive compound, glitter, or sand may be added for additional texture. Several coats of acrylic medium are then applied and are allowed to dry thoroughly.
Next, the artist prints her collagraphs in an "intaglio" process.
Ink is spread over the entire area, and the surface ink is wiped off. The plate is put face-up on an etching press and covered with a damp 100% rag paper. Felt blankets are placed on top, and the plate is passed through the press. Finally, watercolor washes are added to each individual print.

Published by Dial Books for Young Readers
A Division of Penguin Books USA Inc.
375 Hudson Street
New York, New York 10014

Special thanks to Judith Herschlag Muffs, Judaica consultant
Design by Nancy R. Leo
Printed in the U.S.A.
First Edition
1 3 5 7 9 10 8 6 4 2

Library of Congress Cataloging in Publication Data
Silverman, Maida.
My first book of Jewish holidays / Maida Silverman ; collagraphs by Barbara Garrison.
p.   cm.
Summary: An introduction to the ten major holidays of the Jewish people.
ISBN 0-8037-1427-0 — ISBN 0-8037-1428-9 (lib. bdg.)
1. Fasts and feasts—Judaism—Juvenile literature. [1. Fasts and feasts—Judaism.]
I. Garrison, Barbara, ill.   II. Title.
BM690.S497   1994   296.4'3—dc20   93-20370   CIP   AC

For Aaron, Amira, Seth, Talea, Thea—
the newest generation   M.S.

For Sam   B.G.

Two words recur often in this book: "remember" and "imagine." The Torah
tells us that we must "teach our children," a concept that is central to the
religion of the Jewish people. Our history, beliefs, and traditions come alive
for the child who is taught to remember and encouraged to imagine. Just as
memory and imagination link the past to the future, our children are
jeweled links in the precious chain of our heritage.   M.S.

In the Book of Genesis in the Bible, it is written that "God called the light day and the darkness night, and there was evening and morning, one day." This is why, according to the Jewish calendar, the new day begins at sunset.

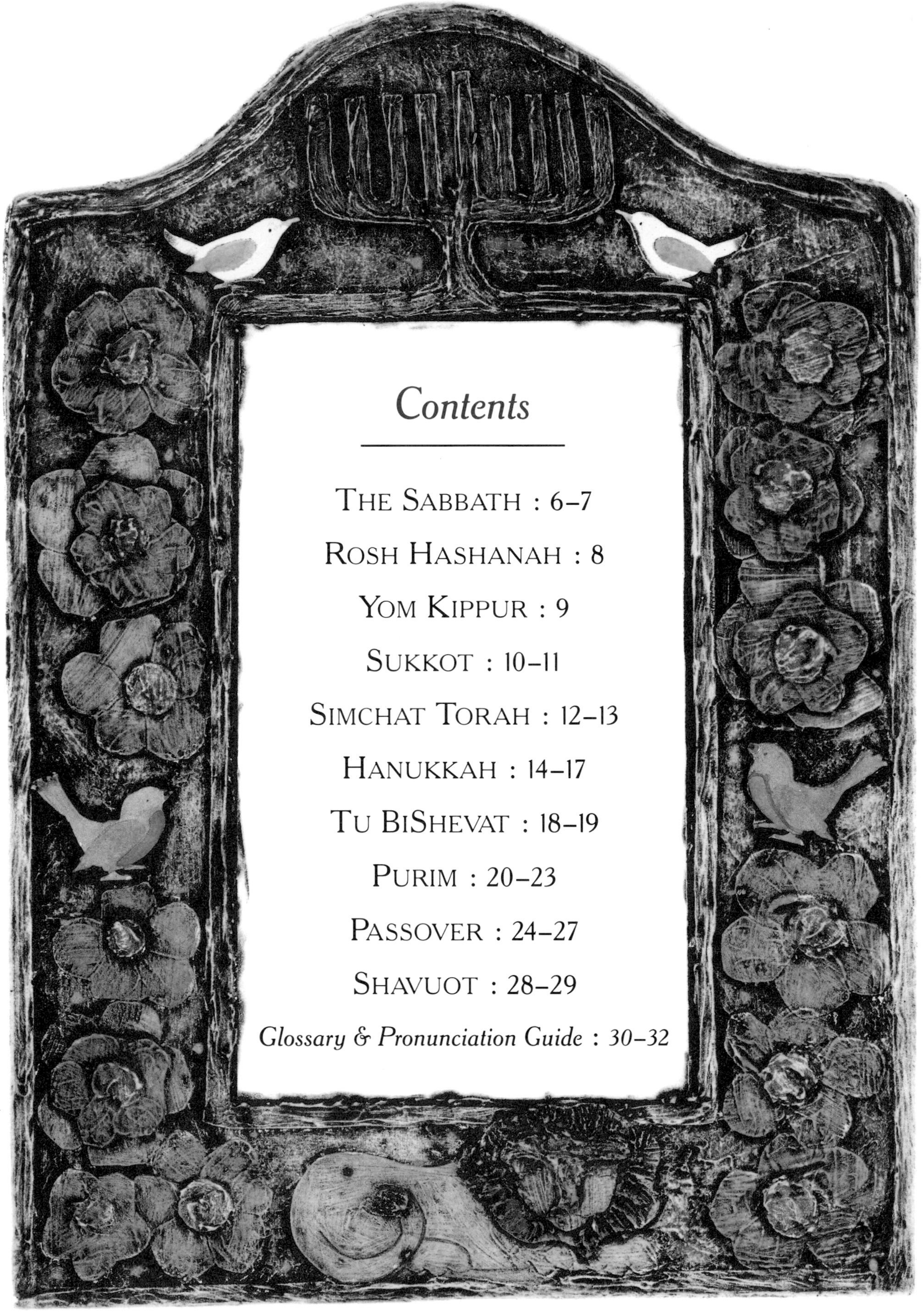

Contents

THE SABBATH : 6–7

ROSH HASHANAH : 8

YOM KIPPUR : 9

SUKKOT : 10–11

SIMCHAT TORAH : 12–13

HANUKKAH : 14–17

TU BISHEVAT : 18–19

PURIM : 20–23

PASSOVER : 24–27

SHAVUOT : 28–29

Glossary & Pronunciation Guide : 30–32

The Sabbath

God created the world in six days. On the seventh day
He rested from the work of creation.
God blessed His day of rest and called it Shabbat—the Sabbath.
He gave the Sabbath to His people as a precious gift.

On Friday the Sabbath arrives with the setting sun.
Before the Sabbath comes,
light the candles! Say the blessing!
Welcome Sabbath as an honored guest—a queen.
We'll greet the Sabbath Queen with joy and gladness.

Come to the Sabbath table!
Thank God for His gift of the vine,
and drink the Sabbath wine.
Thank God for His gift of bread,
and eat the Sabbath loaf.

Saturday is a happy day of rest and peace and joyful prayers.
Tell a story, sing a song! Play a game.
When the sun sets and three stars glitter
in the nighttime sky, Sabbath is over.
Good-bye, beloved Shabbat.
We are sad to see you leave, but we are happy too.
In six days you will return again.

Rosh Hashanah

"Shanah Tovah!" Have a good year!
Rosh Hashanah is the New Year of the Jewish people.

The days of our New Year are holy.
Light the holiday candles and say the prayer:
   "Blessed are You, O Lord our God,
    King of the universe, Who has kept us in life,
    and has preserved us,
    and enabled us to reach this season."

Set the festive New Year table!
Enjoy the New Year feast.
Dip your apple slice in sweet honey and eat it.
May the New Year to come be as sweet as apples and honey.

In the synagogue on Rosh Hashanah
listen to the call of the shofar:
"Tooo-o-o-o!"—a loud, strong sound.
We pray that God will hear it
and give us a sweet New Year of happiness and peace.

Yom Kippur 🌹

Yom Kippur is a very holy day.
No one works or goes to school.
Teenagers and grown-ups do not eat or drink today.
They spend the day praying in the synagogue.

On Yom Kippur remember that God wants us to forgive.
Has someone hurt your feelings?
God hopes you will forgive that person.
Have you hurt someone's feelings?
Are you sorry you did?
Ask that person to forgive you.
God hopes people will be kind to one another
all through the year that is to come.

Sukkot

Long ago when the Jews were slaves in Egypt,
God chose a good man named Moses
to lead them away to freedom.

After they left Egypt,
the Jews lived in the desert
and took shelter in huts called sukkot.
Later when the Jews were farmers,
they gathered the harvest of good things to eat
and thanked God for the foods of the earth.

On Sukkot Jewish people remember the huts in the desert.
We remember God's gifts
and thank Him for a good harvest.
On Sukkot build a hut, a sukkah!
Spread the roof with green branches,
so the moon and stars may shine in.
Decorate the sukkah with vegetables and fruits of the season.
It is beautiful!

Light the holiday candles and say the blessing.
Eat in your sukkah with friends and family.
Hold the lulav and the etrog. Shake them together!
Say a prayer of thanks to God,
who makes all good things grow.

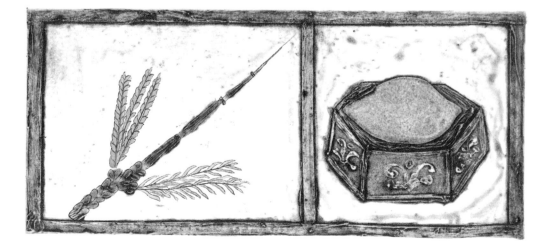

Simchat Torah

Rejoice on Simchat Torah! Today Jewish people
celebrate the Torah, their greatest treasure.

The Torah tells how God created the world.
It tells the story of the Jewish people.
The Torah explains the rules and commandments
God gave His people.

The Torah scrolls are dressed in fine velvet.
Silver crowns adorn them.
The crowns have bells that jingle merrily
as if singing a song in honor of the Torah!

In the synagogue on Simchat Torah
we carry the Torah scrolls in our arms
and march seven times around the synagogue.
Join the happy parade! Wave your flag.
Dance and sing with joy.
Rejoice in the Torah! It is the Tree of Life
to the Jewish people.

Hanukkah

Long ago the Jewish people prayed to God
in the Holy Temple in Jerusalem.
Each day they poured pure olive oil
into the beautiful Temple Menorah,
and lit its seven lamps to honor God.

One day a new king, Antiochus, became ruler of Jerusalem.
"Jews shall not pray to their God," he said.
"They shall pray to my gods of stone, or die!"

The cruel king sent his soldiers to Jerusalem.
They locked the Temple.
Jews could no longer pray there,
or light the golden Menorah.
The Jews refused to pray to stone gods.
They prayed to the One God in secret.

King Antiochus learned of this and was furious!
He sent his army to crush the Jews.
But a brave man named Judah Maccabee
led a small band of fighters to battle
against the king's soldiers.
The Maccabees were greatly outnumbered,
but they fought bravely.
They chased the king's soldiers out of the land.
Judah Maccabee led the Jews back
to the Holy Temple in Jerusalem.

Judah Maccabee searched for oil
to light the lamps of the Temple Menorah.
He found only one jar, enough for just one day.
The Jews lit the Menorah—and God made a miracle!
The oil lasted for eight days,
long enough to make more oil.
The Jews were joyful. They celebrated the miracle
and praised God for helping them
win a great victory over a cruel king.

On Hanukkah we celebrate the miracle of the oil
and Judah Maccabee's victory.
Light the candles in your menorah!
Add a candle, one more for each of the eight nights,
until all the candles are glowing.
Spin your dreidel! Play a dreidel game.
Tell the story of the first Hanukkah.
Remember that long ago God made miracles in Jerusalem.

Tu BiShevat

Jewish people never forget that God created trees.
Jewish people love trees
and honor them with a holiday called Tu BiShevat,
a New Year's Day for trees.

Imagine that you are an apple tree.
Your spring blossoms give sweet nectar
for bees to make into honey.
Birds nest in your branches.
Your strong roots grip the earth,
and wild creatures live safely among them.
When autumn comes,
your leaves turn red, yellow, orange, brown.
They fall and fly away.
Your bare branches dance in winter winds.
Snow is your blanket while you wait for spring.

Plant a little tree on Tu BiShevat.
Care for it so it will thrive.
Happy New Year, trees!
Grow in health each year and prosper,
O trees that beautify the earth.

Purim

"You must bow down to me!"
That was what a man named Haman, the king's advisor,
told a Jew named Mordecai in Persia long ago.
"Never!" Mordecai answered. "Jews bow only to God."
Mordecai's reply made Haman very angry.
"So the Jews won't bow to me.
Then I shall kill them all!" he vowed.

Mordecai learned of Haman's wicked plan.
He hurried to tell his cousin Esther, the Persian queen.
Esther went to tell King Ahasuerus, her husband.
"Haman plans to kill the Jews," she cried.
"I too am Jewish. If my people must die,
I want to die with them!"

King Ahasuerus loved Esther
and was amazed by what she said.
"No Jew has ever harmed me," he answered,
"and Mordecai once saved my life.
Haman is a wicked man," the king told Esther.
"The Jews shall live and *he* shall die!"

It came to pass as the king commanded,
and the Jews of Persia were thankful
that he'd spared their lives.
Brave Queen Esther and Mordecai
declared a special holiday—Purim.

Let's go to the synagogue on Purim!
Listen to the Story of Esther.
Whenever you hear wicked Haman's name,
twirl your grogger. Stamp your feet,
so his name will be blotted out.

Purim is a day for fun!
Wear a costume. Wear a mask.
Join a Purim parade.
Eat hamantaschen. Share some with a friend.
Have a Purim feast!
Be joyful on this happy day.

Passover

Long ago the Jews were not free.
They were slaves of Pharaoh, the Egyptian king.
Pharaoh forced his slaves to build his cities.
They had no time to eat, or rest, or sleep.

The Jews were very sad.
They prayed to God to rescue them.
God heard their prayers.
He chose a wise man named Moses
and told him to lead the Jews out of Egypt.
God made Pharaoh let them go.

At first Pharaoh was glad the Jews had gone.
Then he changed his mind,
and sent his army to bring them back!
Pharaoh's soldiers followed Moses and trapped the Jews
on the shores of the Red Sea.

"God will save us," Moses said.
He stretched his hand over the waters.
The sea rolled back
and the Jews crossed over to the other side.
When Pharaoh's army followed,
Moses stretched out his hand once more.
The sea rushed down and drowned the soldiers.
The Jews were safe and free.

On Passover, or Pesach as it is also called,
Jewish people remember that once
God freed them from slavery in Egypt.
They celebrate with a feast called a seder,
and read the haggadah, a book that tells
the story of Passover.

Imagine that you were a slave in Egypt.
Eat the bitter herb. Dip parsley in salt water and eat it.
Remember that slavery is bitter,
and that Pharaoh's slaves shed tears of sadness
as salty as the water.

Taste the matza,
the flat, unleavened bread Jewish people eat during Passover.
Remember the matzot the Jews baked in haste
when they fled from Egypt,
because they could not wait for the bread to rise.

Sweet wine reminds us that freedom is sweet,
but we do not forget Pharaoh's soldiers.
We are sorry that they drowned
in order for us to be free.
We spill a bit of wine to remember them.

A goblet of wine waits on the seder table.
It is for the prophet Elijah, God's messenger.
Open the door! Let Elijah's spirit enter,
bringing the hope of peace and freedom
for all to share.

Shavuot

Be joyful on Shavuot!
It is the birthday of the Jewish religion.

On Shavuot we remember that Moses, our great leader,
brought the Jews to a mountain called Sinai
in the desert long ago.
Lightning flashed—thunder rumbled.
Clouds and smoke covered the mountain.
It seemed to be on fire.
But Moses was not afraid, for he knew
God had come to the mountain.

Then God revealed Himself to Moses and the Jewish people,
and told them the Ten Commandments.
God's Commandments tell us how God wants us to live,
so that we honor Him and respect each other.

In the synagogue listen to the Ten Commandments
when they are read aloud.
Remember that on this day
God chose the Jewish people from among the nations
to receive His Commandments.

Glossary & Pronunciation Guide

Ahasuerus (A-*ha*-shoo-*air*-us) : A king of ancient Persia; Queen Esther's husband.

Antiochus (An-*tee*-oh-kus) : King of Judea and Jerusalem who began his rule approximately 175 B.C.E.

bitter herb : Horseradish root or a lettuce such as romaine or endive.

dreidel (*dray*-del) : A square top with four Hebrew letters, one on each side, that stand for the words "a great miracle happened there" (in Jerusalem).

Elijah (E-*lie*-jah) : A beloved prophet of the Jewish people.

Esther (*Es*-ter) : A Jewish maiden who married the Persian king Ahasuerus.

etrog (*et*-rog) : A large, fragrant citrus fruit that resembles a lemon. It is used during Sukkot. See also *lulav*.

grogger (*grah*-ger) : A Yiddish word for "noisemaker"; the rattle that children twirl on Purim to drown out Haman's name whenever it is mentioned.

haggadah (ha-*gad*-da) : A book read during the Passover seder that explains the order and observance of the seder ceremony.

Haman (*Hay*-men) : The prime minister to King Ahasuerus of Persia.

hamantaschen (*hah*-man-tash-in) : A three-cornered pastry filled with poppy seeds or fruit jam, eaten during Purim. It is supposed to resemble the shape of Haman's hat.

Hanukkah (*Ha*-noo-kah) : "Hanukkah" means "dedication." During Hanukkah Jewish people celebrate the rededication of the Holy Temple in Jerusalem after Judah Maccabee's victory. The holiday is also called the "Festival of Lights." Hanukkah is celebrated for eight days. The first candle is lit after the sundown that ushers in the twenty-fifth day of the Hebrew month of Kislev (November–December in the civil calendar). Each evening another candle is lit, until all eight are lit after sundown on the second day of Tevet (usually December).

Holy Temple : The building in Jerusalem where Jews worshiped God during Bible times.

Judah Maccabee (*Joo*-da *Mack*-a-bee) : A beloved hero of the Jewish people who drove a tyrant king, Antiochus, out of Jerusalem and the Holy Temple. "Maccabee" means "hammer."

lulav (*loo*-lav) : A palm branch bound together with myrtle and willow branches. Along with the etrog, these "four species" represent all green things that grow. During Sukkot the lulav and etrog are held and a blessing is said over them.

Maccabees (*Mack*-a-bees) : The small band of brave men who with Judah Maccabee hammered at the armies of King Antiochus and defeated them.

matza; plural, **matzot** (*mat*-za, mat-*zote*) : Thin crackerlike cakes made with flour and water only. Jewish people eat matza instead of bread during Passover.

menorah (meh-*no*-rah) : A Hanukkah lamp that may burn candles or oil. During Hanukkah one light is lit for each of the eight days of the holiday. A ninth helper candle is used to light the others.

Mordecai (*Mor*-de-kai) : A great leader of the Jewish people; Queen Esther's cousin.

Moses (*Mo*-ses) : A great leader of the Jewish people. God chose him to lead the Jews out of Egypt.

Passover (*Pass*-o-ver) : This holiday is also called "Pesach," which means "pass over," because God passed over the Jewish people when he smote the firstborn of the Egyptians. Passover is celebrated for eight days, from the fifteenth through the twenty-second of the Hebrew month of Nisan (March–April).

Pharaoh (*Fay*-row) : A name given to ancient Egyptian rulers.

Purim (*Poo*-rim) : The word "purim" comes from the Hebrew word "pur," meaning "lots." Haman cast lots—small stones resembling dice—to decide on a favorable month and day to kill the Jews of Persia. Purim is celebrated on the fourteenth day of the Hebrew month of Adar (February–March). When the Hebrew leap year occurs, there are two Adars and Purim is celebrated on the fourteenth day of Adar II. Jewish people donate money before the holiday so the poor can have a Purim feast too.

Rosh Hashanah (*Rosh* Ha-*sha*-na) : "Rosh Hashanah" means "Head of the Year." According to tradition, it is the birthday of the world—when the world was created. In the Hebrew calendar the holiday is celebrated on the first and second day of Tishri (September–October).

Sabbath : One of the most important Jewish holidays. The Jewish Sabbath is observed from sunset on Friday to after dark on Saturday.

seder (*say*-der) : The special service and meal held on the first and second evenings of Passover. "Seder" comes from a Hebrew word that means "order."

Shabbat (Sha-*baht*) : The Sabbath; from the Hebrew word for "to cease" or "to rest."

Shanah Tovah (*Sha*-na *Toe*-va) : Freely translated from the Hebrew, this means "May you have a good and happy New Year."

Shavuot (Sha-voo-*oat*) : "Shavuot" means "weeks." This holiday is called the "Feast of Weeks" because it arrives seven weeks after the second day of Passover. Shavuot is celebrated on the sixth and seventh days of the Hebrew month of Sivan (May–June). During Bible times Shavuot was a harvest holiday—the Holiday of Ripe Wheat, when Jews brought sheaves of their finest wheat to the Holy Temple in Jerusalem.

shofar (*show*-far) : A trumpet made from a ram's horn. It is sounded in the synagogue during Rosh Hashanah and to signify the end of Yom Kippur.

Simchat Torah (*Sim*-hat *Toe*-rah) : "Simchat Torah," which means "Rejoicing with the Torah," is celebrated on the twenty-third day of the Hebrew month of Tishri (September–October). On this day the last book of the Torah (Deuteronomy) is completed and the reading of the first book (Genesis) is immediately begun. This signifies that Torah study never ends.

sukkah; plural, **sukkot** (*soo*-ka, *soo*-cot) : Small huts that commemorate those the Jewish people dwelled in after they left Egypt and lived in the desert.

Sukkot (*Soo*-cot) : This holiday is also called "Festival of Booths" and "Holiday of Ingathering"; during Bible times Jews gathered the harvest at this season. Sukkot is celebrated from the fifteenth through the twenty-second day of Tishri (September–October).

Temple Menorah : A large seven-branched lamp of gold that stood in the Holy Temple in Jerusalem during Bible times.

Torah (*Toe*-rah) : The first five books of the Bible: Genesis, Exodus, Leviticus, Numbers, and Deuteronomy. The word is sometimes also used to refer to all twenty-four books of Holy Scripture.

Torah scroll : The roll of parchment paper upon which the Torah is handwritten in Hebrew. The scroll is rolled on two wooden rollers, one at each end of the parchment.

Tu BiShevat (*Too* Besh-*vat*) : "Tu BiShevat" means the "fifteenth day of the month of Shevat" (January–February). It is a very important holiday in Israel, where winter has ended and spring is beginning. Israelis of all ages plant hundreds of thousands of young trees, transforming deserts and rocky places into life-giving green lands.

Yom Kippur (*Yom* Kee-*poor*) : "Yom Kippur" means "Day of Atonement" or "Day of Forgiveness." It is the most solemn day of the Jewish year. Yom Kippur is celebrated on the tenth day of Tishri (September–October). The day is spent in the synagogue, fasting and praying. Yom Kippur marks the end of the ten-day period, called the "Days of Repentance," that begins with Rosh Hashanah.